The Song of Songs

The Song of Songs
Which is Solomon's

Illustrated by W. Russell Flint

Gramercy Books
New York · Avenel, New Jersey

Introduction
Copyright © 1993 by Outlet Book Company, Inc.
All rights reserved

This 1993 edition is published by Gramercy Books,
distributed by Outlet Book Company, Inc.
a Random House Company,
40 Engelhard Avenue
Avenel, New Jersey 07001

Random House
New York • Toronto • London • Sydney • Auckland

Designed by Melissa Ring

Printed and bound in Singapore

Library of Congress Cataloging-in-Publication Data
Bible. O.T. Song of Solomon. English. 1993.
Song of songs / illustrated by W. Russell Flint.
p.   cm.
ISBN 0-517-09285-9
I. Flint, William Russell, Sir, 1880–1969. II. Title.
BS1483.F3   1993
223'.905208—dc20   92-39153
                                                CIP

8 7 6 5 4 3 2 1

Introduction

The Song of Songs, also known as *The Song of Solomon* or *The Canticles*, is one of the most beautifully written books of the Old Testament. It is a collection of love poems, spoken alternately by a woman and her beloved, and contains some of the most moving and intimate passages in the Bible.

The author of the book, which belongs to the Writings, the third section of the Hebrew biblical canon, is unknown; Solomon's name was added later. The original lyrics probably had no religious significance, but were, perhaps, frequently sung at wedding celebrations. Although the poems are secular, and there is never any mention of God, according to some scholars they were received into the biblical canon because of their attribution to Solomon and because of their use as wedding songs, since marriage was ordained by God. Other rabbinic scholars believe that these impassioned poems are an allegory of God's love for Israel. Yet other interpretations, according to Christian tradition, are that they are an allegory for the marriage of Christ with the Church or of the individual soul joined with God.

No matter what the interpretation, these poems transcend their theological meaning and radiate the passion and universality of spiritual as well as physical love.

William Russell Flint, the brilliant British artist, created the highly original illustrations in this magnificent edition of *The Song of Songs.*

GAIL HARVEY

New York
1993

The Song of Songs, which is Solomon's

The First Chapter

*L*et him kiss me with the kisses
of his mouth—
For thy love is better than wine.
Thine ointments have a goodly fragrance,
Thy name is as ointment poured forth;
Therefore do the maidens love thee.

Draw me, we will run after thee.
The king hath brought me into his chambers;
We will be glad and rejoice in thee,
We will find thy love more fragrant than wine.
Sincerely do they love thee.

I am dark, but comely,
O ye daughters of Jerusalem,
As the tents of Kedar,
As the curtains of Solomon.
Look not upon me, because I am swarthy,
Because the sun hath tanned me:
My mother's sons were angry with me;
They made me the keeper of the vineyards;
But mine own vineyard have I not kept.

*T*ell me, O thou whom my soul loveth,
Where thou feedest, where thou makest
   thy flock to rest at noon;
For why should I be as one that veileth herself
Beside the flocks of thy companions?

If thou know not, O thou fairest among women,
Go thy way forth by the footsteps of the flock
And feed thy kids beside the shepherds' tents.
I have compared thee, O my love,
To a steed in Pharaoh's chariots.
Thy cheeks are comely with rows of jewels,
Thy neck with chains of gold.
We will make thee circlets of gold
With studs of silver.

While the king sat at his table,
My spikenard sent forth its fragrance.
My beloved is unto me as a bag of myrrh,
That lieth betwixt my breasts.
My beloved is unto me as a cluster of henna
In the vineyards of En-gedi.

Behold, thou art fair, my love; behold, thou art fair;
Thou eyes are as doves.

Behold, thou art fair, my beloved, yea, pleasant;
Also our couch is leafy.

The beams of our houses are cedar,
And our rafters of cypresses.

The Second Chapter

I am a rose of Sharon,
A lily of the valleys.

As a lily among thorns,
So is my love among the daughters.

As an apple tree among the trees
    of the wood,
So is my beloved among the youths.

I delight to sit in his shadow
And his fruit is sweet to my taste.
He brought me to the banqueting house,
And his banner of love was over me.

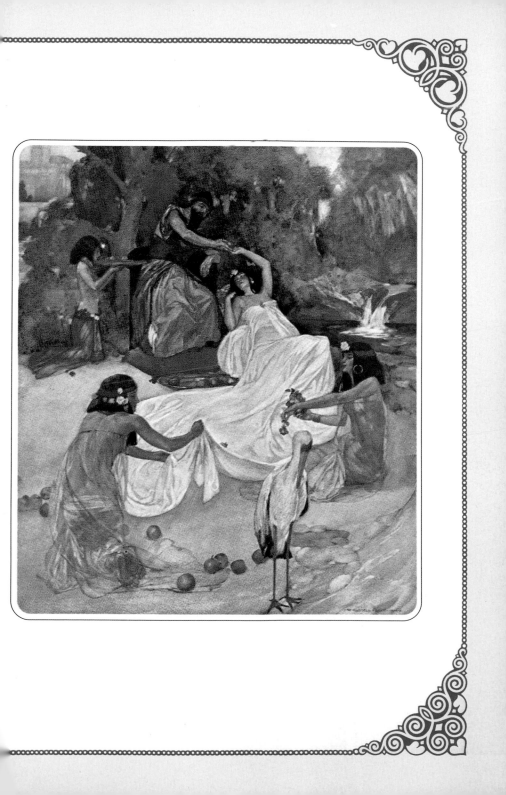

Stay me with flagons, comfort me with apples;
For I am lovesick.
His left hand is under my head,
And his right hand doth embrace me.

I adjure you, O daughters of Jerusalem,
By the gazelles, and by the hinds of the field,
That ye stir not up, nor awake my love,
Till he please.

The voice of my beloved!
Behold, he cometh
Leaping upon the mountains,
Skipping upon the hills.
My beloved is like a gazelle or a young hart:
Behold, he standeth behind our wall,
He looketh in through the windows,
He peereth through the lattice.
My beloved spoke, and said unto me:

"Rise up, my love, my fair one, and come away.
For, lo, the winter is past,
The rain is over and gone;
The flowers appear on the earth;
The time of singing is come,
And the voice of the turtle is heard in our land;
The fig tree putteth forth her green figs,
And the vines in blossom give forth
 their fragrance.
Arise, my love, my fair one, and come away.

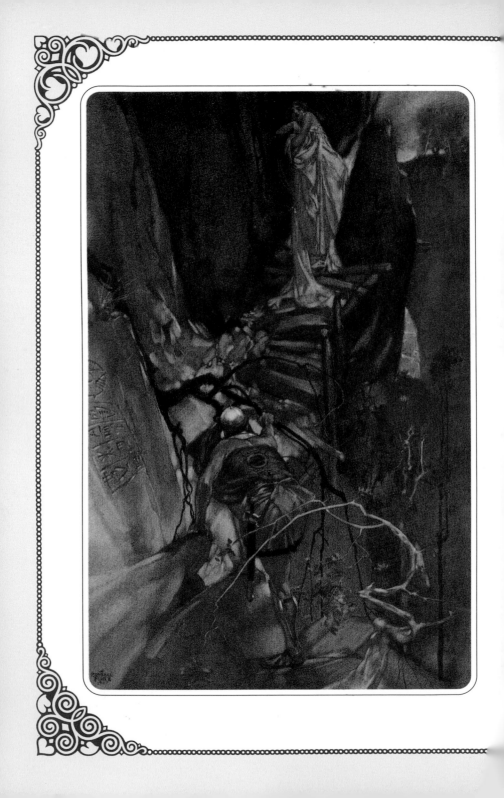

O my dove, that art in the clefts of the rock,
In the covert of the cliff.
Let me see thy countenance, let me hear thy voice;
For sweet is thy voice,
And thy countenance is comely.

Take us the foxes,
The little foxes, that spoil the vineyards;
For our vineyards are in blossom."

*M*y beloved is mine, and I am his,
That feedeth among the lilies.

Until the day break, and the shadows flee away,
Turn, my beloved,
And be thou like a gazelle or a young hart
Upon the mountains of spices.

The Third Chapter

*B*y night on my bed I sought him whom
   my soul loveth;
I sought him, but I found him not.
I will rise now, and go about the city;
In the streets, and in the broad ways,
I will seek him whom my soul loveth.
I sought him, but I found him not.
The watchmen that go about the city found me:
To whom I said, "Saw ye him whom my soul loveth?"
Scarce had I passed from them,
But I found him whom my soul loveth:
I held him, and would not let him go,
Until I had brought him into my mother's house,
And into the chamber of her that conceived me.

I adjure you, O daughters of Jerusalem,
By the gazelles, and by the hinds of the field,
That ye awaken not, nor stir up love,
Until it please.

Who is this that cometh up out of the wilderness
Like pillars of smoke,
Perfumed with myrrh and frankincense,
With all powders of the merchant?
Behold, it is the litter of Solomon;
Threescore valiant men are about it,
Of the mighty men of Israel.
They all hold swords, being expert in war:
Every man hath his sword upon his thigh
Because of dread in the night.

King Solomon made himself a palanquin
of the wood of Lebanon.
He made the pillars thereof of silver,
The bottom thereof of gold,
The seat of it of purple,
The inside thereof being paved with love,
From the daughters of Jerusalem.

Go forth, O ye daughters of Zion,
And gaze upon King Solomon
With the crown wherewith his mother crowned him
On the day of his wedding,
And on the day of the gladness of his heart.

The Fourth Chapter

*B*ehold, thou art fair, my love; behold, thou art fair;
Thine eyes are as doves behind thy veil;
Thy hair is as a flock of goats,
That trail down from Mount Gilead.
Thy teeth are like a flock of ewes all shaped alike,
Which came up from the washing;
Whereof all are paired,
And none faileth among them.
Thy lips are like a thread of scarlet,
And thy mouth is comely:
Thy temples are like a pomegranate split open
    behind thy veil.
Thy neck is like the tower of David
Builded with turrets,
Whereon there hang a thousand shields,
All the armor of the mighty men.

Thy two breasts are like two fawns
That are twins of a gazelle,
Which feed among the lilies.

Until the day break,
And the shadows flee away,
I will get me to the mountain of myrrh,
And to the hill of frankincense.

Thou art all fair, my love,
And there is no spot in thee.

*C*ome with me from Lebanon, my bride,
With me from Lebanon:
Look from the top of Amana,
From the top of Shenir and Hermon,
From the lions' dens,
From the mountains of the leopards.

Thou hast ravished my heart, my sister, my bride;
Thou hast ravished my heart with one of thine eyes,
With one bead of thy necklace.

How fair is thy love, my sister, my bride!
How much better is thy love than wine!
And the smell of thine ointments than
  all manner of spices!

Thy lips, O my bride, drop honey—
Honey and milk are under thy tongue;
And the smell of thy garments is like
the smell of Lebanon.

A garden enclosed is my sister, my bride;
A spring shut up, a fountain sealed.
Thy plants are an orchard of pomegranates,
With precious fruits;
Henna, with spikenard plants,
Spikenard and saffron,
Calamus and cinnamon,
With all trees of frankincense;
Myrrh and aloes, with all the chief spices.
Thou art a fountain of gardens, a well
  of living waters,
And flowing streams from Lebanon.

*A*wake, O north wind;
And come, thou south;
Blow upon my garden,
That the spices thereof may flow out.
Let my beloved come into his garden,
And eat his pleasant fruits.

The Fifth Chapter

I am come into my garden, my sister, my bride:
I have gathered my myrrh with my spice;
I have eaten my honeycomb with my honey;
I have drunk my wine with my milk:
Eat, O friends;
Drink, yea, drink abundantly, O beloved.

I sleep, but my heart waketh:
Hark: my beloved knocketh, saying,
"Open to me, my sister, my love,
My dove, my undefiled:
For my head is filled with dew,
And my locks with the drops of the night."

I have put off my coat;
How shall I put it on?
I have washed my feet; how shall I defile them?
My beloved put in his hand by the hole of the door,
And my heart was moved for him.

I rose up to open to my beloved;
And my hands dropped with myrrh,
And my fingers, flowing myrrh,
Upon the handles of the lock.

I opened to my beloved;
But my beloved had turned away,
    and was gone:
My soul failed when he spoke.
I sought him, but I could not find him;

I called him, but he gave me no answer.
The watchmen that went about the city found me,
They smote me, they wounded me;
The keepers of the walls took my mantle from me.

I adjure you, O daughters of Jerusalem,
If ye find my beloved,
That ye tell him, that I am lovesick.

What is thy beloved more than another beloved,
O thou fairest among women?
What is thy beloved more than another beloved,
    that thou dost so adjure us?

My beloved is clear-skinned and ruddy,
Preeminent among ten thousand.
His head is as the finest gold,
His locks are curled, and black as a raven.
His eyes are as the eyes of doves by the rivers of waters,
Washed with milk, and fitly set.
His cheeks are as a bed of spices, as banks of sweet herbs;
His lips are like lilies, dropping with flowing myrrh.
His hands are as rods of gold set with the beryl:
His body is as polished ivory overlaid with sapphires.
His legs are as pillars of marble,
Set upon sockets of fine gold:
He is as majestic as Lebanon,
Stately as the cedars.
His mouth is most sweet:
Yea, he is altogether lovely.
This is my beloved, and this is my friend,
O daughters of Jerusalem.

The Sixth Chapter

Whither is thy beloved gone,
O thou fairest among women?
Whither hast thy beloved turned him?
That we may seek him with thee.

My beloved is gone down to his garden,
To the beds of spices,
To feed in the gardens, and to gather lilies.
I am my beloved's, and my beloved is mine:
He feedeth among the lilies.

*T*hou art beautiful, O my love, as Tirzah,
Comely as Jerusalem,
Terrible as an army with banners.

Turn away thine eyes from me, for they have
   overcome me.
Thy hair is as a flock of goats that trail down from
   Gilead.
Thy teeth are as a flock of ewes which are come up from
   the washing,
Whereof all are paired, and none faileth among them.
Thy temples are like a pomegranate split open
Behind thy veil.

There are threescore queens,
And fourscore concubines,
And maidens without number.
My dove, my undefiled, is but one;
She is the only one of her mother,
She is the choice one of her that bore her.

The daughters saw her, and called her happy;
Yea, the queens and the concubines,
    and they praised her.

Who is she that looketh forth as the dawn,
Fair as the moon, clear as the sun,
And terrible as an army with banners?

I went down into the garden of nuts
To look at the green plants of the valley,
And to see whether the vine budded,
And the pomegranates were in flower.

Before I was aware, my soul set me
Upon the chariots of Ammi-nadib.

The Seventh Chapter

*R*eturn, return, O Shulammite;
Return, return, that we may look upon thee.
What will ye see in the Shulammite?
As it were a dance of two companies.

How beautiful are thy steps in sandals,
O prince's daughter!
The roundings of thy thighs are like jewels,
The work of the hands of a skilled workman.
Thy navel is like a round goblet,
Wherein no mingled wine is wanting.
Thy belly is like an heap of wheat
Set about with lilies.
Thy two breasts are like two young fawns
That are twins of a gazelle.
Thy neck is as a tower of ivory;

Thine eyes as the pools in Heshbon,
By the gate of Bath-rabbim:
Thy nose is like the tower of Lebanon
Which looketh toward Damascus.
Thine head upon thee is like Carmel,
And the hair of thy head like purple;
A king is held captive in the tresses.

How fair and how pleasant art thou,
O love, for delights!

This thy stature is like to a palm tree,
And thy breasts to clusters of grapes.
I said, I will go up into the palm tree,
I will take hold of its branches;

And let thy breasts be as clusters of the vine,
And the fragrance of thy breath like apples;
And thy mouth like the best wine
That glideth down sweetly for my beloved,
Moving gently the lips of those that are asleep.

I am my beloved's,
And his desire is toward me.

*C*ome, my beloved, let us go forth into the field;
Let us lodge in the villages.

Let us get up early to the vineyards;
Let us see if the vine has flowered,
Whether the blossoms have opened,
And the pomegranates be in flower;
There will I give thee my love.
The mandrakes give forth fragrance,
And at our doors are all manner of precious fruits,
New and old,
Which I have laid up for thee, O my beloved.

The Eighth Chapter

O that thou wert as my brother,
That sucked the breasts of my mother!
When I should find thee without, I would kiss thee;
Yea, and none would despise me.

I would lead thee, and bring thee
Into my mother's house,
That thou mightest instruct me;
I would cause thee to drink of spiced wine
Of the juice of my pomegranate.

His left hand should be under my head,
And his right hand should embrace me.

I adjure you, O daughters of Jerusalem,
That ye stir not up, nor awake my love, until he please.

Who is this that cometh up from the wilderness,
Leaning upon her beloved?

Under the apple tree I awakened thee;
There thy mother brought thee forth:
There she that bore thee brought thee forth.

*S*et me as a seal upon thine heart,
As a seal upon thine arm;
For love is strong as death,
Jealousy is cruel as the grave;
The flashes thereof are flashes of fire,
Which hath a most vehement flame.
Many waters cannot quench love,
Neither can the floods drown it;
If a man would give all the substance of his house
   for love,
He would utterly be contemned.

*W*e have a little sister,
And she hath no breasts;
What shall we do for our sister
In the day when she shall be spoken for?
If she be a wall,
We will build upon it a turret of silver:
And if she be a door,
We will enclose her with boards of cedar.

I am a wall,
And my breasts like the towers thereof;
Then was I in his eyes
As one that found peace.

Solomon had a vineyard at Baal-hamon;
He gave over the vineyard unto keepers;
Every one for the fruit thereof
Brought in a thousand pieces of silver.

My vineyard, which is mine, is before me:
Thou, O Solomon, shalt have the thousand,
And those that keep the fruit thereof two hundred.

Thou that dwellest in the gardens,
The companions hearken to thy voice:
"Cause me to hear it."

Make haste, my beloved,
And be thou like to a gazelle
or to a young hart
Upon the mountains of spices.